DISCARDED
Fordham University Libraries

IMMEDIATE MAN
CUIMHNÍ AR CHEARBHALL Ó DÁLAIGH

ISBN 0 85105 416 1

Edited by Aidan Carl Mathews

IMMEDIATE MAN
CUIMHNÍ AR
CHEARBHALL Ó DÁLAIGH

DR. ISAAC COHEN
CYRIL CUSACK
PAUL DURCAN
BRENDAN KENNELLY
THOMAS KINSELLA
SIOBHÁN MC KENNA
AIDAN CARL MATHEWS
JOHN MONTAGUE
TOM MURPHY
EIBHLÍN NÍ BHRIAIN
MÁIRTÍN Ó DÍREÁIN
BREANDÁN Ó HEITHIR
PÁDRAIG Ó FIANNACHTA
RORY O'HANLON
BRENDAN SMITH

frontispiece by LOUIS LE BROCQUY

1983
THE DOLMEN PRESS

IMMEDIATE MAN is designed by Liam Miller, set in Palatino type by Redsetter Limited in Dublin, and printed in the Republic of Ireland by The Leinster Leader Ltd., Naas, for the publishers,

THE DOLMEN PRESS
Mountrath, Portlaoise, Ireland

June 1983

The edition consists of:

125 special copies, signed by the editor and bound in boards, of which 100 are for sale [ISBN 0 85105 417 x];

1000 standard copies [ISBN 0 85105 416 1].

© 1983 The Dolmen Press Limited, all rights reserved.

CONTENTS

Democratic Concretes *by* Aidan Carl Mathews 9
My Friend the President *by* Cyril Cusack 15
Immediate Man *by* Brendan Kennelly 21
A Court in Session *by* Rory O'Hanlon 23
Cúig Céimeanna na Síoraíochta
  by Pádraig Ó Fiannachta 37
Transcendent Cleanliness *by* Tom Murphy 41
Cearbhall Ó Dálaigh *by* Máirtín Ó Direáin 45
Cuimhní ar Chearbhaill Ó Dálaigh
  by Breandán Ó hEithir 47
Two Swans *by* Aidan Carl Mathews 51
Fear ar Rothar *by* Eibhlín Ní Bhriain 53
An Bonnán Buí / The Yellow Bittern
  by Thomas Kinsella 55
Community Spirit *by* Isaac Cohen 59
A Resigned President *by* John Montague 63
The Great Tent has Collapsed *by* Brendan Smith 65
Lament for Cearbhall Ó Dálaigh *by* Paul Durcan 69
Not the Finish but Rebirth *by* Siobhán McKenna 73

Chronology 77
The Memorial 79

Frontispiece by Louis le Brocquy

strata iacent passim sub quaeque sub arbore poma
(Everywhere the fruit lies strewn under its parent tree)

Virgil, *Ecologues* vii, 54

AIDAN CARL MATHEWS

DEMOCRATIC CONCRETES

It is a nice irony that Cearbhall Ó Dálaigh would have been surprised and embarrassed by this book of tributes. He was not himself an ironist, because irony is so often a stratagem of prevention, and Ó Dálaigh lived a wholly unprevented life. Still, he could be whimsical when occasion did *not* permit it, and I imagine that his talent for drollery would have been exercised on this volume. He would have thought it excessive and undeserved. His openness to the worth and vulnerability of others had nothing in it of the severity he trained upon himself.

To say these things is to speak in the mode of paradox. That too is fitting. Ó Dálaigh was himself a paradox: his goodness manifest, its source inscrutable. He was a Judge whose life was modelled on that of a man sentenced by due process to a criminal's death. He was a public figure who cherished privacy; an individualist who was selfless; a critic of established values who revered the sapience of institutions; a patrician who was at ease among very plain folk. Most of all, he was a man of peace; we acknowledged this, in our own queer way, by giving him a military funeral.

But these are decent ambiguities, through which his great good sense — tactful yet forthright — carried him safely. He never confused the search for excellence with the quest for good, nor flukes of success with acts of achievement. Frugal in his personal habits, innocent in his preferences, he was a sophisticate, a figure in salons, a Maecenas who disliked both emperors and empires. An amorous man, he was in love with the world, but without the least tincture of worldliness; a plainspoken man, his whole life was a reply to the bare hands with Greek and Latin. Most crucially (a word he loved), he was an extraordinary man because he was more ordinary than the rest of us.

How may one best remember him? He was a jurist, a poet, a rider of horses, a scholar, a journalist, a liturgist, a lover driven to clearheaded gaiety and excited tenderness by a world he found to be festive, almost Ovidian in its plenitude. I can see him sitting among children on a swing-seat in a red verandah, reading from a book of Japanese legends, a matador's hat perched on his head; and I see him, again among the young, pushing buttons on a pinball machine, with that casual intensity of his, late at night in a café bar on the main road out of Luxembourg.

Pictures. Many of them, none blurred. In one, he is stepping from his State car in Kerry to make room during a rainstorm for a half-mad geriatric, a Johnny Fortycoats; and slipping off that evening to provide, from his own pocket, for a new dwelling, a helping hand, an electrical connection, running water. Again, I recall him in his chambers, mischievous among the terrible volumes of proscript and penalty, at work upon smallprint in search of a subsection that might pluck a thorough wrongdoer from jail.

I can hear his voice too, now that I listen, the same clear accent on the telephone, gladly urgent: "Do you happen to remember what Cosimo de Medici said when he first saw Fra Angelico's predella of the San Marco altarpiece?" Impish notes from the Chinese mainland capture his intonation, at once affectionate and donnish: "The Great Helmsman has been misunderstood".

Two years later, I found him bearded — almost venerable, a mandarin — in his iron hospital bed, a convalescent who was concerned only that visitors dine at his expense in a local hotel, and drink mulled wine against the sleets of January. That one time, he was dejected: but even his dejection was ergetic, directed. I thought then of the Chinese character for a man: a force in a field, a strength in motion.

Let us remember him for the present as a beekeeper. I delight to think of him wading up the garden in his protective clothing, encumbered and solid among the snap-dragons and the red hot pokers, an astronaut bearing honey in his gloved hands. Of his many skills, that of the apiarist most wryly characterises him, this man who eludes, baffles, exasperates us. He had mastered an art which, more so than most, demands of its practitioner long increments of labour, attentiveness, solicitude, and which rewards him in due course by granting him a rare and privileged delicacy, a produce so mysterious and sweet that the ancients placed its cultivation under the tutelage of a god.

Yet the beekeeper remains masked, in costume, a persona. How then can we be sure of a near likeness in our talk of him? Setting these varied tributes in a semblance of order, I have been struck, time and again, by a certain recurrent idiom, an unforeseen accord among the contributors in their use of descriptive terms: "eagerness", "spontaneity", "gladness", "confidence", "expectancy", "absorption", such words. Were I to add any others, I might choose *gratitude* and *astonishment*. Cearbhall found it easy to thank — his devotion to the Christian eucharist is only a specialised instance of that capacity; and he was perpetually in the state of wonder. In classical terms, (few others are so contemporary), he was a man not only of *pietas* and of *gravitas*, but also of *hilaritas*. His own zest for accurate language and proper names is a case in point. He relished the power of speech, not from any Adamic motive of authority, but because it meant he could talk to other people. *Elementary Yoruba, Basic Urdu, Intermediate Portuguese, Conversing in Serbo-Croatian* . . . . many such odd booklets littered his bureau, proof of a gift for intimacy, a desire to make greeting and take leave in as many of Babel's dialects as could be brought to book in the space of a lifetime.

Ten years ago at least, Cearbhall gave me a copy of Whitman's *Specimen Days in America*. He had always loved that rowdy, ludic man shouting his hymns to the copula; and admired no less the murdered President whom Whitman mourns in his book. Indeed, the poet's celebration of Lincoln is matched in strength only by the aplomb with which he dismisses Edgar Allan Poe, that man of wilful gloom and obstructed loyalties. With an almost forensic grandeur, Whitman deplores Poe's "abnegation of the perennial and democratic concretes". This may seem a trifle lofty; in fact, it's straight talk. Cearbhall would have liked it, would have noted it. Not surprisingly, when I turn to the book (I have it still) to mark the passage, I find the job done. Cearbhall's asterisk is there before me, star-shaped, as if he were mapping new-found bodies, fresh and further light in the nightsky of the mind.

We can know so much about him, and no more. That summer before Yom Kippur, when things were different, I went with Cearbhall to view, and to pray in, the cathedral of Chartres. From the outside, the lead-framed apertures loured darkly among titanic growths of masonry. Within, the window-spaces blazed in a host of colours, radiant, placid, heavy with the life of sunlight striking through azure and vermilion. "Much like the person", Cearbhall hinted. "The exterior blank, resistant, uncourted; inside, rich and voluptuous colour, the hidden treasure of the self, unknown to others, at moments withheld from itself. When you come upon it, you realise in the same instant that you stand in the presence of God". Let us leave the matter there.

Cearbhall is five years dead. To the hiddenness of self, he has added the final secrecy of the perfect tense. On a certain morning in late winter (he would have said in early spring), he was grateful for the last time, tender for the last time, roguish for the last time. Since then, many well-meaning persons have lamented his death, but the talk is wild, done in the world's terms. It is not so much that one is happy he was spared the debility and grievance of old age — his, in any case, would have been abundant; nor that he had completed his life's work, whatever that bizarre formulation may be thought to express; nor that his death was tragic, since it inspired no pity or terror. There is not even a question of sadness at his being cut off. Instead, we should be glad that he died as he had lived — *in medias res*, at the start of a day's work. Besides, he had practised dying all his life. The manner of his departure only increases our joy in him, because his death, no less eloquently than his life, exposes the past tense as a grammatical makeshift. Were his friends to die, his detractors to keep silent, his books to be immured, his judgments to be reversed, his taqpes scrubbed, his home levelled, and his grave obliterated, Cearbhall Ó Dálaigh would remain a presence. His life was lived in that faith, his faith in that life.

Let us say then that he was a man who lived by two

touchstones, two exorbitant ways of understanding. He believed, in the first instance, that men and women were made in the image and likeness of god; and he added, or drew from, this impractical conviction the logical corollary that he should therefore cherish his neighbour. Accordingly, he was a man of almost subversive charity who reminded us in his least action not only of what we might be, but of what we are.

I have his yarmulka, his books, poems, letters, notelets, cufflinks, shirts, shoes, clothes horse; and, in a time of fearless mediocrity, the structuring force of his example. I have as well a promise made to him, and still unfulfilled: that I translate in hexameters a poem by the Vichy minister, Robert Brassilach, entitled "Le Jugement des Juges", The Judgment of the Judges. In it, the condemned collaborator, awaiting the hour of his death in Fresnes prison, anticipates a final tribunal at which the exalted of this world will foregather to be accused, indicted, and arraigned by the destitute and abandoned multitudes, the utter of the earth. I can still hear Cearbhall saying "Dedicate it to me, if you would; I suspect it may be very much like that on the last day . . ."

He need not have worried. A man who fed the starving, clothed the naked, visited those in prison, suffered for those in pain, laughed for those in joy, a man who brought us honey from a lost hive, will surely be among those who are called blessed.

CYRIL CUSACK

MY FRIEND THE PRESIDENT

There was a flurry of movement along the platform, and a sibilance rising in crescendo sounding like "ssta pressd!", which, translated by my daughter Niamh, became — "It's the President!"

A group of plainclothes men suddenly burst through a bulge in the crowd. A bright-faced, fur-hatted gentleman appeared, smiling, eyes shining — my friend the President.

I seem to be viewing my friend in a rushing stream of vigorously living vignettes.

Here now, in a railway station more resembling an opera-house, came Cearbhall, slotting through the big-boned bodyguard.

Bird-like, spotting us, "An dtiocfaidh sibh isteach sa chathair liom?", he said, offering a lift. He always had an affection for our wayfaring profession; had he not, in College days, played the part of Napoleon in Shaw's playlet, *The Man of Destiny*? Then, addressing the daughter, "Cionnas atá tú, a Niaimh?", he asked, and I remembered that they had once had a great talk together at the Royal Irish Academy of Music. The limousine stood waiting. Deferentially the big fellows cleared a way. But better we should excuse ourselves. Already we had the pleasure of being made feel important.

Homing towards Hatch Street, along the quays we dawdled with the evening light.

"Let's cross over", I said.

So, crossing Grattan Bridge, held up by the gasping green metal sea-urchins, we could twist a way through back-streets and alley-ways towards the South Circular, the grand after-school parade, and with the great names, Grattan, Emmet, Pearse — and Ó Dálaigh — trumpeting bugle-notes in the head, come on to Synge Street.

"That's where he went to school", I said, pointing to a sturdy-looking building, a house of granite jutting forth authority, a school for the breeding of ideals, reformist zeal and rebel parliaments, buttressed and abetted, maybe, by a chuckling cherub from a few yards down the street, at No. 33 — the birthplace of George Bernard Shaw.

I am certain that my friend, the President, slipped into long trousers before I did. His were of a dark tweed, rumpled yet adding to his general purposefulness. He was of that rare class of boy before whom the others hesitated to swear, not from any chivalrous fear of shocking but because, with Cearbhall, an obscenity would be like a pebble dropped against a granite cliff — ineffectual.

Coming on to holiday-time, bags strapped to our backs or swinging belted packs of schoolbooks, members of our class would saunter, kicking up puffs of summer dust, along the banks of the Royal Canal. Standing by the small Venetian bridge, we would watch the little lads, naked, splashing about in the leafy water. Then you could notice our friend, under a tree perhaps, eyes to the grass in frowning concentration or upward-turned towards the Dublin hills — until observed, when, with a quick, bird-like turn of the head, would come the sudden smile, rueful, almost apologetic.

My memory telescopes on to the great green acres of Phoenix Park and our football battles there; then, switching over the Liffey, to Croke Park and that long-ago Leinster Schools Final of the Gaelic game. And we won, Cearbhall, we won.

Down a street or two, turn back an autumn leaf or two, and there this day of spring, pink-veiled by cherry blossom, lay the old University college in Earlsfort Terrace.

"I think", I said to my daughter, "we became more aware of people in the days here . . ."

We became more self-aware, others more aware of us, largely through College clubs and societies and with brave contemporary spirits, like the little revolutionary poet, hardly the height of a rifle, Charles Donnelly, "the Shelley of U.C.D.", soon to die in the Spanish Civil War; the sharp-toothed satirist, Brian Ua Nualláin; poets Devlin and Donagh MacDonagh, son of the executed 1916 leader; novelist Mary Lavin, and many others. There seemed to be no part of College life in which Cearbhall was not engaged — the Intervarsity Republican Club, the Cumann Gaelach, the Literary and Historical — the famous L & H — at "86", site of Cardinal Newman's University in St. Stephen's Green.

Today, the once busy Main Hall was emptied of the life and excitement and the sometime frivolity of those early years.

"Once upon a time", I went on with the tale, "we were evicted from the Main Hall".

The Officers Training Corps had been formed, and there was to be a demonstration against any such soldiering with the official requirement of an Oath of Allegiance to the British Crown. As we gathered in the Main Hall, we were suddenly confronted by the bulky figure of Dr. Conway, Vice President of the College, and given a curt dismissal. I remember the look of bright expectancy on Cearbhall's face as, with Con Lehane, later elected to the Dáil for Clann na Poblachta, Sean McBride's party, and Frank Ryan, then Editor of An Phoblacht, and a small group of supporters, we retreated to Cathal Brugha Street, a popular venue for political protest, and there staged our meeting before a sprinkling of curious Dubliners.

I have the impression that he took even our simple escapades in all seriousness. He would gladly engage in the College Rag, but not as an indulgence in trivial anarchy — like the frivolous invasion of some city theatre; instead, it would be as a contribution to a cause. Once, with less charity perhaps, we took a cinema by storm — with more of thunder than lightning — our future President participating, but this was by way of protest at the showing of a sentimental film seen as an impudent reflection on things Irish. For Ó Dálaigh nothing was unworthy bar the triviality of injustice.

Sunday mornings, then, might find him with the Walking Club, complete with stick, starting out from the Church in Rathfarnham to walk the mountains . . . voices chattering down the dusk of evening until, with lights springing up from the city below, they dropped into silence and memory.

Already, from schooldays, we were alert to the enviable simplicity of spirit discernible in Cearbhall, to an earnestness of purpose, no poor thing prematurely coffined in egoism and self-serve but a part of the national purpose aching for its proper place of growth.

Yet, on a personal note touching certain youthful confidences, these he met with a reserved, at times somewhat puzzled, concern. I recall, on his appointment as Irish Editor to the Irish Press, myself desiring to impress a red-haired, Rossetti-like lady of the Irish Jewish community. Presumptuously, I wrote a plea, all too relevant, for racial and religious tolerance. With patience and scholarly expertise, an accent here and an aspirate there, my kindly editor converted the apologia into decent Gaelic. In later years, catching sight of our President on a visit to the synagogue, I wondered did he hear some small echo of that juvenile voice.

My memory attaches itself most to the L & H (where perhaps he most revealed himself) and to those tempestuous meetings at No. 86, with such as Maud Gonne McBride, her cathedral-like figure trailing black draperies to the Chair; Professor Maguinness, reputed to surpass Lloyd George in rhetoric; and revolutionaries like Frank Ryan and Helena Moloney, the politician John Dillon, Dr. J. C. Flood and Michael Farrell, with Brian Ua Nualláin, black prince of hecklers, standing at the door.

Now stands the Auditor, flinging out argument, afire, agitated but never angry. Mental agility without disguise, deviousness or opportunism, made Ó Dálaigh a formidable opponent in debate: honorable, even vulnerable, but always indomitable. As devastating a weapon as any was, I believe, the momentary hesitation with puckered brow which came from a sense of fairness, his willingness to take a point; seconds after, with that bird-like adroitness, he could hop on a strongly supporting twig to see the adversary tumble.

Here was a leading light in College, a light dancing and darting out and about the brazen images of disenchantment, dazzling the shadows back into obscurity, not only with words but with sheer honesty of presence: the "eternal student", eager-eyed, excitedly seeking renewal and, even through the lowering pall of experience, seeing all things as new.

A kindred spirit with the actor and the humble patron of

the Irish stage, his elevation to the Presidency was a joy for the theatrical profession. Almost within hours of the Inauguration at Dublin Castle, President Ó Dálaigh was hot-foot down to the National Theatre for a first performance of *The Vicar of Wakefield* and remembrance of Goldsmith, the Trinity sizarship boy. Whether or not, as a sometime student player in the College Dramatic Society, Cearbhall fully shared the Shavian brand of humour, I can still savour his rendition of the famous "Napoleon" speech in *The Man of Destiny*:

". . . the English are a race apart. No Englishman is too low to have scruples; no Englishman is high enough to escape from their tyranny . . . When he wants a thing, he never tells himself that he wants it. He waits patiently until there comes into his mind, no one knows how, a burning conviction that it is his moral and religious duty to conquer those who possess the thing he wants . . . He is never at a loss for an effective moral attitude. . ."

I was privileged to be present at the Castle ceremony and, given short notice during a theatre rehearsal, I arrived self-consciously in civilian dress — the line of church dignatories and elder statesmen seeming to me oddly stooped and "theatrical" — to stand beside our old teacher, Brother Mullen, bristling with pride as our mutual friend, grave and palefaced but still carrying the grace of boyhood, moved slowly towards the rostrum. The address at one point, touching contemporaries of the past, returned me to our days at U.C.D. . . .

A stream of vignettes, I said . . . Cearbhall the schoolboy, the undergraduate, auditor, adult student at the Italian Institute; with Frank Aiken, in the balcony of the Royal Irish Academy of Music; chatting in Irish with my daughter at the Shelbourne; Attorney-General, European judge, President . . . and always with that look of eager absorption and expectancy.

My friend withdrew from office on the 22nd of October, 1976. Soon after — too soon for us — he withdrew from this life.

BRENDAN KENNELLY

IMMEDIATE MAN

If, in the course of a journey
That covers more than half a country,
Small though that country be,
And there is this opportunity

To see, as if for the first time,
Lakes that glint back at you for a name,
Fields that together create a wild home
Till the world is a particular room,

A child thirsts because all this
Is bigger and deeper than anything she knows
Or can know during years stretching like stations
Ahead of her into treachery and promise

Mingling,
Is it not a heart-lifting
Sight to see a laughing
Prince of a man rising

From his seat in a crowded train
And go, immediate man,
To return with solace for one
Who, undistressed in a moment, will never forget him?

"The fields and the lakes have names, dear,
And every rock, mountain and hill,
And don't worry if the stations come quickly or slowly
Or there are too many hurrying people.

Take your ease and consider them all,
Think of the names and know what you feel."
He gets off at Killarney, this man of style.
Over the years, she has mentioned his smile,

His greyhound words, his wise eyes,
His contemplative hands' impulsive ways,
The sense he transmitted that we are witnesses
To stations, fields, lakes we should name and praise.

RORY O'HANLON

A COURT IN SESSION

Cearbhall Ó Dálaigh is best remembered among lawyers for his unique contribution to the development of constitutional law in Ireland. His period as Attorney General extended from the late 1940s to 1953, at which stage he was appointed a Judge of the Supreme Court without being required to serve the customary apprenticeship in the High Court. He became Chief Justice in 1961 and presided over the Supreme Court for twelve years, until his appointment to the Court of Justice of the European Communities towards the end of 1972.

The significance of his era as President of the Supreme Court can best be appreciated by placing it in contrast with the decades which preceded it. From the foundation of the State in 1922 until the enactment of the new Constitution in 1937, the basic constitutional document was the Constitution of the Irish Free State (Saorstát Éireann) Act, 1922. enacted by Dáil Éireann sitting as a Constituent Assembly. As an instrument for the protection and guarantee of human rights it had one inherent weakness — that for a period of eight years (later extended to sixteen years) it could be amended by simple Act of the Oireachtas. Furthermore, the courts tended to take the view that if any Act of the Oireachtas passed during that period proved inconsistent with the terms of the Constitution, then the Constitution was deemed to have been amended — albeit accidentally and unintentionally — by the passing of the Act in question. Not surprisingly, therefore, this first Constitution of the new State made little impact in the field of human rights, and the constitutional problems with which the High Court and supreme Court had to grapple during the 1922-1937 period were mainly concerned with questions of the legality of disengagement from links with the Crown, the termination of the right of appeal to the

Privy Council, and other matters deriving from the significance of the Treaty as part of our constitutional framework.

All that changed after the enactment by the people of the Constitution of 1937, but the radical changes which took place in the field of constitutional law did not happen overnight, and it seems open to doubt whether they were ever foreseen or intended by Mr. De Valera in his capacity as principal architect of the new structure.

Having grown accustomed over a period of many years to a situation in which they could do little or nothing to control the powers of the Legislature, the courts were slow to take on their new role of custodians of the constitutionally-guaranteed rights of the citizen which had been given them by Bunreacht na hÉireann, and a policy of severe judicial self-restraint appears to characterise the reported decisions on constitutional matters for about twenty years after the new Bill of Rights had been thrust into their hands.

During that period several attempts were made to challenge legislation as being repugnant to the guarantees contained in the Constitution, but almost uniformly without success. This is not to say that any particular decision of the High Court or the Supreme Court was incorrect, but many of the judgments were couched in language which gave little encouragement for the future to those who hoped that the new Constitution would be a more effective instrument to safeguard their rights and liberties than had been the document of 1922.

The exceptions were few and far between. In 1943 the Supreme Court ruled against the School Attendance Bill, 1942, which had been referred to the Court by the President under Article 26 of the Constitution, and in doing so the Court vindicated the right and duty of parents to provide for the education of their children in such manner as they thought proper, subject to their obligation to ensure that the child received a certain minimum education. In 1947 the Court rejected as unconstitutional part of the Trade Union Act, 1941, on the basis that it infringed the right of the citizen to join the trade union of his choice, or to refrain from joining any trade union if he chose to do so. In 1950, the Supreme Court condemned the Sinn Féin Funds Act,

1947, as being repugnant to the Constitution on two different grounds — first as contravening the property rights of the Plaintiffs, who sued as trustees of the Sinn Féin organisation, and secondly, as amounting to an unconstitutional interference by the Oireachtas in the judicial domain reserved to the Courts by the express terms of the Constitution.

These decisions, coupled with the trenchant condemnation of internment without trial which was contained in the judgment of Gavan Duffy J. in *The State (Burke) v. Lennon* in 1940, were almost the only cases in which, for a period of twenty years and upwards after its enactment, the Constitution was invoked successfully by any litigant as a stated guarantee of his fundamental rights which neither Legislature nor Executive could override.

The manner in which constitutional law flowered and developed in the decade which followed was all the more remarkable for the rather arid period which had preceded it. People now began to think of the Constitution as a potent instrument for the protection of their personal rights against oppressive conduct on the part of the State or of powerful interests other than the State itself.

This new chapter in an important field of Irish law may be regarded as having commenced with the successful challenge to part of the Solicitors' Act, 1954, in proceedings leading to a judgment of the Supreme Court delivered in 1958, at a time when Cearbhall Ó Dálaigh was a member of the court but had not yet become Chief Justice. The court was unanimous in the view that the power to strike a Solicitor off the rolls formed part of the administration of justice, and was of too serious a character to entrust to a professional body, having regard to the constitutional provisions regarding the function of the courts.

This was the first of a series of cases in which the High Court and Supreme Court jealously safeguarded the principle of the separation of powers of government which underlies the Constitution. In 1963 the Supreme Court under the Presidency of its new Chief Justice, Cearbhall Ó Dálaigh, again asserted the primacy of the courts in the judicial domain in a case where the Revenue Commissioners sought to exercise their statutory right to fix the amount of the penalty in relation to customs offences. The judgment of the Court contains a good example of the clear and forceful style of the Chief Justice, and illustrates vividly his concern for the protection of the citizen against any excessive use of the powers of the State.[1]

> Where the Legislature has prescribed a range of penalties the individual citizen who has committed an offence is safeguarded from the Executive's displeasure by the choice of penalty being in the determination of an independent judge. The individual citizen needs the safeguard of the Courts in the assessment of punishment as much as on his trial for the offence. The degree of punishment which a particular citizen is to undergo for an offence is a matter vitally affecting his liberty; and it is inconceivable to my mind that a Constitution which is broadly based on the doctrine of the separation of powers . . . could have intended to place in the hands of the Executive the power to select the punishment to be undergone by citizens. It would not be too strong to characterise such a system of government as one of arbitrary power.

He returned to the same theme in the later case of *The State (C) v. Minister for Justice,* 1967)[2]. A prisoner on remand who was found to be insane while awaiting trial was, under a statute of 1875, to be detained in a mental institution until the Lord Lieutenant directed him to be brought before the court again. A similar power was claimed for the Minister of Justice as successor to certain functions of the Lord Lieutenant. The argument was rejected out of hand by the Chief Justice in the following terms:

> In the year 1875 it was for an omnipotent parliament to determine what should be done in the case of a prisoner on remand who was discovered to be insane; no question could arise as to whether the provision made by parliament was or was not an intrusion into the judicial domain. It is otherwise now because the Constitution effects a separation of legislative, executive and judicial powers. Cases and circumstances will undoubtedly occur in which the lines dividing these several areas of government are difficult to discern; but in my opinion there is little room for debate as to the area in which a prisoner on remand is to be placed. He stands well within the

clearly-marked borders of the judicial domain .... The
provision of the Act of 1875 (which takes the accused
away from the Court's disposal, sets at naught the
Court's remand, and adjourns the preliminary
investigation *sine die*) is about as large an intrusion
upon a court proceeding as one could imagine .... it is
for the court that has seisin of a criminal matter to
determine whether or not the accused is suffering from
insanity of such a character as renders him unfit to
stand his trial.

The same general approach to the function of the courts
under the new Constitution was visible in the dissenting
judgment given by Cearbhall Ó Dálaigh, as an ordinary
member of the Supreme Court, in *Melling v. Ó
Mathghamhna,* (1962)[3], where he commenced his judgment
by giving expression to some general observations:

> If our Constitution and the Constitution of Saorstát
> Éireann both have adopted the theory of the tripartite
> separation of the powers of government with express
> limitations on the power alike of Legislature and
> Executive over the citizen, the reason is not
> unconnected with our previous experience under an
> alien government whose parliament was omnipotent
> and in whose executive lay wide reserves of prerogative
> power. It is therefore not surprising that it was thought
> right to place certain rights beyond the reach of both the
> Legislature and the Executive, and among these is the
> right of trial by jury, for ordinary citizens, in ordinary
> circumstances, of all criminal charges which are not
> minor offences .... The alternative tribunal which the
> law allows a citizen in the case of a criminal charge
> which is not a minor offence is a jury, whose members
> are wholly independent of executive or legislative
> discipline or displeasure and who by their very
> numbers bring to the administration of justice the
> commoner touch .... The safeguard of trial by jury is
> against an improbable but not-to-be-overlooked
> future; and it is for this reason the Constitution
> enshrines it.

Two other cases, however, mark the outstanding
contribution of Cearbhall Ó Dálaigh as Chief Justice, to the

development of constitutional jurisprudence in Ireland. The first of these was *The State (Quinn) v. Ryan*, (1965)[4], where the Supreme Court had to consider afresh two previous decisions of the Court confirming the validity of Sec. 29 of the Petty Sessions (Ireland) Act, 1851, when considered in the light of the Irish Free State Constitution, and later when reviewed again after the enactment of the Constituton of 1937. This was the Section which permitted the "backing" of English warrants for arrest within the jurisdiction of the Irish courts, so as to enable persons charged with offences to be arrested and brought back to England to face trial. In both of the earlier cases the procedure had been upheld, but in Quinn's case the facts demonstrated that the police powers could be used in such a way as to enable a suspect to be spirited out of the jurisdiction before he had an opportunity to challenge the validity of his arrest before the Irish courts. Enquiries by Quinn's legal representatives as to his whereabouts proved fruitless. An application to the High Court for habeas corpus was refused by a strong Divisional Court of three judges presided over by Davitt P. The Supreme Court, however, presided over by Chief Justice Ó Dálaigh, had no hesitation in declaring the whole procedure a gross breach of the prisoner's constitutional rights. In one of his most hard-hitting judgments the Chief Justice spelled out clearly that any Act which permitted a citizen to be cut off from his constitutional right of access to the courts to vindicate his personal rights, could not survive the test of constitutional challenge. Having reviewed the facts of the case, he said:

> From this survey of the evidence, it becomes clear that a plan was laid by the police, Irish and British, to remove the prosecutor after his arrest on the new warrant from the area of jurisdiction of our Courts with such dispatch that he would have no opportunity whatever of questioning the validity of the warrant. It is also clear that the applicant's solicitor was refused information (and in one instance supplied with misinformation) as to his client's whereabouts while his client was still within the jurisdiction, and that this refusal was persisted in while the prosecutor was still in Northern Ireland.

In plain language, the purpose of the police plan was to eliminate the Courts and to defeat the rule of law as a factor in Government . . . The claim made on behalf of the police to be entitled to arrest a citizen and forthwith to bundle him out of the jurisdiction before he has an opportunity of considering his rights is the negation of law and a denial of justice.

It was not the intention of the Constitution in guaranteeing the fundamental rights of the citizen that these rights should be set at naught or circumvented. The intention was that rights of substance were being assured to the individual and that the Courts were the custodians of these rights. As a necessary corollary it follows that no one can with impunity set these rights at naught or circumvent them, and that the Courts' powers in this regard are as ample as the defence of the Constitution requires. Anyone who sets himself such a course is guilty of contempt of the Courts and is punishable accordingly.

This case is of considerable interest since there was no apparent conflict between the old provisions of the Petty Sessions Act and the new Constitution, and it had successfully withstood challenge on a number of previous occasions. Ultimately, however, on an examination of what was *intra vires* the Act, the Supreme Court came to the conclusion that it could be used in such a way as to thwart implied rights guaranteed by the Constitution, and therefore that it should be regarded as inconsistent with the Constitution.

A similar rather radical approach may be detected in the second major judgment of Cearbhall Ó Dálaigh, as Chief Justice, which has already been referred to. This came in the case of *In re Haughey*, (1971)[5], which arose out of the failure by Padraic Haughey to answer questions before the Dáil Éireann Committee of Public Accounts concerning the expenditure of Grant-in-Aid moneys for Northern Ireland. His refusal to do so was based on the fact that serious allegations had been made against him by other witnesses under the protection of statutory immunity, and that he had not been permitted to cross-examine them by his counsel, or to have his counsel address the Committee in his own defence. When prosecuted for his refusal to answer before the Committee, the stand taken by him was upheld by the Supreme Court. The judgment of Chief Justice Ó Dálaigh, representing the decision of the majority of the Court, contains the following passage[6]:

> No court is unaware that the right of an accused person to defend himself adds to the length of the proceedings. But the Constitution guarantees that the State "so far as practicable" (sa mhéid gur féidir é) will by its laws safeguard and vindicate the citizen's good name. Where, as here, it is considered necessary to grant immunity to witnesses appearing before a tribunal, then a person whose conduct is impugned as part of the subject-matter of the inquiry must be afforded reasonable means of defending himself . . . Without the two rights which the Committee's procedures have purported to exclude, no accused — I speak within the context of the terms of the inquiry — could hope to make any adequate defence of his good name. To deny such rights is, in an ancestral adage, a classic case of *clocha ceangailte agus madraí scaoilte*. Article 40, Section 3, of the Constitution is a guarantee to the citizen of basic fairness of procedures. The Constitution guarantees such fairness and it is the duty of the Court to underline that the words of Article 40, Section 3 are not political shibboleths but provide a positive protection for the citizen and his good name.
>
> The provisions of Article 38, section 1, of the Constitution apply only to trials of criminal charges . . . but in proceedings before any tribunal where a party to the proceedings is on risk of having his good name, or his person or property, or any of his personal rights jeopardised, the proceedings may be correctly classed as proceedings which may affect his rights, and in compliance with the Constitution the State, either by its enactments or through the Courts, must outlaw any procedures which will restrict or prevent the party concerned from vindicating these rights.

The grand sweep of this declaration of human rights under the Constitution has led to its being cited perhaps more frequently than any other judicial pronouncement in later cases where new parties have come forward to assert claims before the courts in reliance on the basic law of the

State.

Another case which illustrates vividly the concern of the Chief Justice for the fundamental rights of the individual was *The People (Attorney General) v. O'Callaghan,* (1966)[7], where the rules to be applied in relation to release on bail were spelt out in a definitive manner by the Supreme Court. A practice had grown up of opposing bail on the ground that the accused man might use his period of freedom on bail to commit further crimes. In a momentous judgment, Chief Justice Ó Dálaigh castigated this approach to the problem, saying:

> The reasoning underlying this submission is, in my opinion, a denial of the whole basis of our system of law. It transcends respect for the requirement that a man shall be considered innocent until he is found guilty and seeks to punish him in respect of crimes neither completed nor attempted. I say "punish", for deprivation of liberty must be considered a punishment unless it can be required to ensure that an accused person will stand his trial when called upon.
>
> Leaving aside such matters as the likelihood of an accused interfering with witnesses or attempting to destroy evidence if granted bail, it must be borne in mind that the single question in all bail applications is:- Is the applicant likely to stand his trial? If he is, then he should be granted bail and set at liberty ... The Courts owe more than verbal respect to the principle that punishment begins after conviction, and that every man is deemed to be innocent until tried and duly found guilty.

With this central and crucial part of his judgment, the other members of the Supreme Court concurred. But the Chief Justice would have gone further and ruled out the practice on bail applications of giving evidence about previous convictions of the accused — "I could not see how a fair trial could be assured to an accused person if, before his trial, there was a discussion in public Court of this topic". In relation to this aspect of the matter he failed to win the support of his fellow judges.

O'Callaghan's case has caused much heart-searching on the part of successive Governments ever since the judgment was delivered; and the Executive has made no secret of the fact that it would prefer to give much wider scope to the Courts to refuse bail than would be permissible in the light of the Supreme Court's decision. However, although the enactment of special legislation for this purpose has been mooted time and again, it has never come to fruition — the Constitution would make it exceedingly difficult to produce a different result to that which has flown from the dictum of the Judges.

Even this short review of some of the outstanding judgments of Cearbhall Ó Dálaigh in his capacity as Chief Justice may suffice to give an insight into the calibre of the man, and to illustrate his outstanding contribution to the development of Constitutional Law in Ireland in our time. One of the beneficial results which has flown from his willingness to interpret and implement the Constitution in a humane and enlightened manner has been the arousal of great public interest in the topic and the awakening of public consciousness of the protection guaranteed to the life, person, good name and property rights of every citizen. This achievement may be compared to that of Chief Justice Marshall and other dominant figures in the United States Supreme Court, who, by their work of interpretation and exposition, made the American Constitution a very real force in the ordinary life of the people. In the picturesque words of Bernard Schwartz in his work, *American Constitutional Law*:

> At the first sound of a new argument over the United States Constitution and its interpretation, the hearts of Americans leap with a fearful joy. The blood stirs powerfully in their veins and a new lustre brightens their eyes. Like King Harry's men before Harfleur, "They stand like greyhounds in the slips, straining upon the start".

Cearbhall Ó Dálaigh, by his constant insistence on justice and fair procedures, and by the recognition he gave to the concepts of dignity and freedom of the individual which are enshrined in the Constitution, awakened the public consciousness of the rule of law in much the same way. In the process, the Constitution ceased to be a sterile legal text, reserved for academic debate among lawyers and scholars, and has become instead a powerful living force in the life of the ordinary people of Ireland.

Cearbhall's well-known commitment to the Irish language, culture and traditions was reflected in the pithy phrase with which he summed up the case for the State in *Re Haughey* — "clocha ceangailte agus madraí scaoilte" ("stones tied down and dogs let loose"). In another civil action for damages concerning a horse which was being transported by air and caused a certain amount of havoc in the process, the court had to consider whether the best steps had been taken to deal with the situation, and the Chief Justice again found that an Irish adage contained the best exposition of the problem — "an gad is giorra don scorna a scaoileadh ar dtúis" ("release first the knot that is nearest the throat")! When sitting as a member of the Court of the European Communities in Luxembourg, he was intrigued by the Community rule that the party bringing proceedings which found their way into that lofty tribunal had the choice of the language in which the case was to be conducted. As Irish is one of the recognised languages of the Community he looked forward eagerly to the day when some Irish litigant would avail of the privilege of shedding some Gaelic light on the dark places of the Common Agricultural Policy.

Legal and linguistic systems meet in many different ways. A splendid example of cross-border co-operation is to be found in a little-known work on Irish place-names — the joint authors being Cearbhall Ó Dálaigh and Lord McDermott, then Lord Chief Justice of Northern Ireland. The English text was largely the work of Lord McDermott with the expertise in the Irish language coming from the Príomh Breitheamh.

Possibly the last judgment delivered by him as Chief Justice before his departure to Luxembourg was in the (unreported) case of *Tormey v. Commissioners for Public Works*. It was obviously a case which fired his imagination, for it concerned the acquisition of the Hill of Tara so that its great historical and archaeological treasures could be preserved unharmed for posterity. The power to acquire the land compulsorily depended on the construction to be placed on the terminology of the National Monuments Act, 1930. Could 57 acres of agricultural land be fairly described as a monument? The Court decided that the entire area was a "national monument" within the meaning of the Act. It is worth quoting in full the closing passage in the judgment of the Chief Justice as a vignette to illustrate the qualities of culture, learning, and generosity of spirit which he brought to his 12-year Presidency over the highest tribunal in the land. It runs as follows:

> It will not, I hope, be out of place to call attention to the fact that this is not the first time a land-owner was disturbed at Tara. One of the archaeological sites at Tara is traditionally known as Cormac's house; it lies within Ráth na Ríogh. The building of the great vallum which surrounds Ráth na Ríogh is, by tradition, ascribed to Cormac, the renowned MacAirt. The tradition is that he built it on land belonging to one, Odran, who protested loudly when Cormac began to stake out his work. When the day came for the king to take possession of the house, Odran set his back against the door to prevent the king from entering. The king turned Odran's wrath away with the softest answers conceivable. He promised to compensate him by paying him his own weight in silver, daily rations for a household of nine persons for so long as the king should live, and land of equivalent value elsewhere. Today, Cormac's successors, the Commissioners of Public Works, must pay compensation for extending themselves at Tara, (rightly as I hold) just as Cormac did. All I would add is this. The Commissioners, when they come to negotiate terms of compensation with the dispossessed owner whose lands today abut on Ráth na Ríogh, might bear in mind that, while they do not command royal wealth or unlimited discretion, a niggardly spirit is foreign to the genius and tradition of Cormac Mac Airt, Tara's greatest king, whom historians (according to Macalister) loved to compare to Solomon.

For the practitioner appearing in the Supreme Court during the period of Cearbhall Ó Dálaigh's Presidency, the impression always conveyed was one of unfailing courtesy coupled with firmness of purpose. For a period, there was a vogue among members of the prison population — perhaps encouraged by the well-known concern of the Chief Justice for the protection of human rights — to apply in person to the High Court and Supreme Court to quash their convictions on various technical grounds. One could not but be impressed by the patience and politeness with which many unmeritorious applications of this kind were treated by the Chief Justice. The prisoner was never "Jones" — he was "Mr. Jones", no matter how villainous his appearance or how grim his record.

On one such occasion an unusual difficulty arose. The Chief Justice wished to consult a leading text-book on criminal law in the course of the case, but found himself in the somewhat embarrassing position of having to borrow it from the prisoner who was presenting his case. The litigant had written from prison to ask for books to be made available so that he could become learned in the law before the hearing, and the Chief Justice had — characteristically — directed that his own copy of the text should be released for the purpose.

As a judge, as a person, as a friend, he was a man of outstanding qualities.

1. 1963 I.R., p. 183.
2. 1967 I.R. 106, p. 115.
3. 1962 I.R. 1, p. 39.
4. 1965 I.R. 70, p. 117.
5. 1971 I.R. 217.
6. ibid, p. 263/264.

PÁDRAIG Ó FIANNACHTA

CÚIG CÉIMEANNA NA SÍORAÍOCHTA

1. SAN ACADAMH RÍOGA

Buille clois — a haon, a dó, a trí,
Go poncúil riamh a bhís,
Saothar breithiúnais arna chomhlíonadh
Agus cúraimí na córa curtha go beacht i gcrích.
Níor chuir tú isteach orainn
Ag teacht go cneasta inár measc
Ar do bharraicíní d'fhonn ná scaipfeá
Brothall diamhair an léinn
Le barr urraime dár n-oghamchraobh.

Do chuirtheá gliondar orainn
Mar nach rabhais dall ar ár léann
Is nárbh le Uistínín ná Grotius féin
A bhí ag stiúradh cearta Gael
Ach Ceannfhaela na Foghlama
Is breithiúna an Fhéineachas amhra,
Is an Iodh Morainn gur luigh go seabhrach
Ina mhuince is ní mar rabhadh duit.

2. I GCILL CHOMHAID

An bhainis rí nuair bhí le comóradh,
D'fhillis go lách i measc do chomharsan.
Chuiris tuairisc an othair bhí id chóngar
Is bhainis scailp den chroí a bhí leonta.
Nuair nach gceadófaí Aifreann sollónta
Rinneadh cúiteamh ag do chairde is do pharóiste.
Cuireadh breithiúna diagaithe na hEorpa
Faoi dhraíocht ag creideamh an chaoinchomhraic
Nuair a tháinig Íosa chun na bainse i gCill Chomhaid
Is cheiliúir na Dálaigh dá gcomharba.

3. I GCUAN ANNA

Ní raibh coinne agat linn
Ach tú ag ullmhú chun cruinnithe
Ionar ghá iomlán do fhuinnimh cinn.
Go maith Dia dúinn é
Is go maithe Máirín
Mar do ghlaois isteach orainn
Is chuiris scéimh na fáilte
Ar cheannaithe na himní.
Chun boird libh do chuiris sinn
Is roinn orainn bhur lón féin.
Mholais linn ár saothar
Ár n-iarrachtaí don bhriotaireacht Ghaeilge

"Sea, caithfeadsa feasta imeacht
Agus tá Máirín liomsa ag teacht.
Ach fanaigí mar a bhfuil agaibh
I gceannas ar threabh is teach".
Quis custodet ipsos custodes?
"Tá cúraimí stáit orm.
Tugaigí a gcuid don dá mhadra"
Agus ghuíomar an rath ar do bhóthar
Is an tsaoirse agus an chóir go gcosnófá.

4. I DTRÁ LÍ

Bhí do shaothar curtha i gcrích
Gan flaitheas Éireann i gcló caillí.
Bhí an deachú agat á díol
Agus ualach dá réir ar do chroí
Ach Giolla na Fulaingthe le do thaoibh.
Ba rogha leat ceartas fíor
Ná togha an ghradaim rí.

5. I MAOL AN GHALLÁIN

Guígh chun Dé orainn
Cé nach fiú sinn é anois —
Agus nár thángamar go léir ar
Do shocraid mar a d'éalaigh
An Tóibítghrá Gaelach
Is an náire shaolta?
Nár aithníomar an tréith úd
A rinne díotsa lao dúinn
Le hofráil suas chun Dé mhóir
Mar íobairt bhoinn reacht Éireann?

Le teacht faoi dheoidh an tSamhraidh
Beidh an nóinín is an samhaircín,
An deor Dé is an leamhach buí
Faoi bhláth mar choróin sa teampall
A bheidh againn mar Theamhair rí
Mar gur róimh é ag do shamhailse
Go buile cloig an domhainstaid.

TOM MURPHY

CEARBHALL Ó DÁLAIGH: TRANSCENDENT CLEANLINESS

The first time I met Cearbhall Ó Dálaigh I did not know who he was. The face was familiar, shining, but I did not have a name for it. He was then Chief Justice and President of the Supreme Court. (I had been going my self-centred way and living in Camden Town for a number of years). The occasion was a first night of a play of mine, some ten or fifteen minutes before curtain up.

For the writer — any playwright will tell you — these moments are fraught with anxiety, insecurity and dread; were the mind to be able to collect itself and give voice to its panic, I think it would say "My God, what have I done?" Complex motives conspire on these occasions to maintain the writer in his singular, abject state. Those few friends who come forward, ostensibly to offer greetings, are really approaching to search the author's eye for a clue as to the extent of the travesty about to be performed; soon they are backing away gauchely, asking one another is there time for another drink. Those who do not approach appear to know already what the dreadful outcome is to be, the shiftiness of their eyes, their loud hysterical chattering and laughter only too well testifying to this. The actors are shivering backstage, pale under make-up, and the director has gone off to change into a dark suit.

On such an occasion then, the appearance of Cearbhall Ó Dálaigh, whom I did not know, was like an apparition: the arrival was sudden, the movement energetic and purposeful, the hand already outstretched while he yet approached, the enthusiasm unquestionable, support for an effort no matter what the outcome. A presence to assault insecurity. Then the warm handshake and a greeting in Irish, as to a dear friend; best wishes, bilingual, and the shining face was gone. All very brief, but a ministering spirit. A shining face, a transcendent cleanliness, a clear conscience.

Another ministering spirit, and also nameless to me at the time, was Seamus Wilmot. He, too, would appear at some stage, though in different style. Seamus would "happen" to be beside you, his greeting and well-wishing avuncular in gentle understanding.

Those brief encounters helped enormously and left the playwright less morbidly self-centred.

Contemporary dramatists having plays done at the Abbey ten or twelve years ago had that first night sense of isolation compounded by the mystery as to who, or what exactly was the management. Who was putting on the play? It ws rumoured that it was something called a Board; it was said that this Board lived all together, and permanently, on the top floor of the Abbey building; it was understood that all of them were grey, that they were seen only occasionally and, then, only on matters to do with Synge, O'Casey and Yeats. I vowed that if ever I had any kind of official status at the Abbey Theatre I would buy a spotted dickie-bow and attend all first nights by living Irish playwrights, and try to emulate the example of Cearbhall Ó Dálaigh and Seamus Wilmot. (I never rose to the personal quirk of a spotted dickie-bow, but I attend first nights as far as possible).

Of course — as I found later — Seamus Wilmot was a member of the Board of Directors and Cearbhall Ó Dálaigh was a Shareholder (a Trustee) of the Abbey Theatre. And neither of them was grey; both were pleasantly bald.

As one got to know Cearbhall Ó Dálaigh one became increasingly amazed at the extent of his interests and achievements. He spoke many languages and had a particular interest in Italian and French, he had a degree in Celtic Studies, he was Irish Editor of the *Irish Press* newspaper for nearly a decade; he served on Commissions dealing with the diverse subjects of Taxation, Students, Higher Education, Cultural Relations, Alcoholism. The list of his special interests included Refugee problems, public international law, Irish literature, art, education, theatre.

Strikingly, most of those interests and pursuits apply to our first President, Douglas Hyde. Indeed, Douglas Hyde, who was another great linguist, but who "dreamed in

Irish", was also a Doctor of Laws. And both were dedicated in their support of the Arts.

I have said nothing about Cearbhall Ó Dálaigh's distinguished career in Law, his first calling; that is best described by his colleague. I would simply add that simultaneous with his rise from high office to the highest in the land, his generous personality became more manifest and accessible.

When he became President in 1974 his personal attention to the Arts became more evident. He opened the new Project Arts Centre, he visited art exhibitions, he attended book launchings, his presence in theatres was frequent and regular. It was not unusual for him to take in two shows of an evening during the Dublin Theatre Festival. Paintings by contemporary Irish painters hung in Aras an Uachtaráin, others — a stack of them — lay waiting to be framed to take their places on the walls of his residence. People in all walks of the Arts wrote to him about their projects, problems, fund-raising and whatnot, and his response was constructive, caring and understanding.

His knowledge of the great classicists is often commented on. Perhaps more impressive was his familiarity with the works of obscure and minor figures from the past. This kind of discovery would be made when he joined one of those aftermath groups who form at the end of public functions to discuss their specialist subjects: as the conversation continued, the delighted surprise grew at the extent of the President's knowledge. Most appealing of all, I think of his question, "Do you know the work of — ?" And he would supply the name and fill you in with details of some aspiring poet, painter, musician or composer from some corner of the country who had found no larger public, as yet, than one made up of a domestic circle of friends and the President.

An incidental, but a recurring one, which always comes up when Cearbhall Ó Dálaigh's attendance at the theatre is mentioned: the remark, "And did you know he always paid for his tickets?" I did know, and I would have thought that the gesture was simply a further evidence of his support joined with an awareness of the financial strait in which theatre is constantly foundering. But the remark appears to have a deeper meaning for, more often than not, it is attended by a wise face, a shrewd nod and a wink. I regret I cannot plumb the deeper meaning. On one or two occasions I have heard the self-same remark attended by a downcast, doleful expression: I have understood this to mean that the observer, clearly, was feeling sad that, in matters of perks-of-the-trade, the President was not a cute man. But the other attitude is most enigmatic.

He liked to tell the story of the remark he heard one day from a little boy who was standing in a gathering which had stopped to watch the Presidential car drive away: the boy looked at the President in wonder, then up at his mother and asked, "Is that the prisoner, mammy?" Beneath the laughter, Cearbhall Ó Dálaigh was too sensitive a person not to be aware of the truth in the child's slip of the tongue.

He knew that Office can diminish and vitiate personality and create the effect of distance; and the public, too, can become rigid and aloof in its consciousness of the proprieties to do with meeting Office. He was determined that neither would happen. He wanted to meet the general public and he did not wait upon protocol to do so. The single aspect above all others which marked his interpretation of the role of President was informality. It was not achieved effortlessly, or simply on the dictates of a warm and generous nature. He was a reflective and deeply religious man and there ws deliberation, courage, hard work, and true humility in his bringing the Presidency to the people.

The stories of his informality abound and they are remembered with affection: they are too numerous to recount. In any case, a litany of anecdotes — no more than a parade of effusion — cannot convey the warmth in dignity, dignity in informality, informality suffused with nobleness of mind; a celebration of life, the example of a President. And, alas, for too short a time.

MÁIRTÍN Ó DÍREÁIN

DO CHEARBHALL Ó DÁLAIGH

I ngeamhuair chrua na bliana
Thriall an bás aniar ort:
Cuairt d'fhág bior an fhuaicht sáite
I gcroí do mhná is do cháirde.

Lá d'adhlachtha chuisnigh an dúlra,
Tháinig sioc, sneachta, is fuarlach,
Ach d'fhoráil fós le hómós
Gur bán bheadh an poll dubh.

Fuair tusa bua le meabhair is foghlaim,
Is má bhí plána follas go dlúth ort,
'Sé Dia a chuir ort ó thús é,
Is níor ghallmaisíocht ba chúis leis.

Níorbh aon bhuidire tusa
A bheireadh breith go réidh uait,
Ach breitheamh a bheireadh ceartas
Don trua is don tréan uait.

Id' Phríomh-Bhreitheamh Éireann
Is ar chúirt na hEórpa dá éis sin,
Nó arís id' uachtarán críche
Shiúil leat dínit is séimhe.

A ridire uasail an niachais,
Ó d'éagais d'éag an tréith sin,
A shruith-fhir shéimh na humhaile
A fuair ansacht is gnaoi ó dhaoine.

A shéimh-fhir ar gheal leat cleacht is dán.
Dá mb'fhéidir le do cháirde
Fál a chur leis an mbás
Do cháin leis go brách ní íocfá.

A chara an dáin is na dáimhe
Is na dána ionanna a áireamh:
Tusa i ndáil do cháirde
Ba chrann taca gach lá dóibh.

Solas an dáin ní práinn dod' cháil,
Tusa a chin ó aos dána;
Ach glac a chara leis an gcloch seo
A leagaim ar do charn le dúthracht.

BREANDÁN ÓHEITHIR

CUIMHNÍ AR
CHEARBHALL Ó DÁLAIGH

Cé gurbh é "Scéala Éireann" an chéad nuachtán laethúil a chonaic mé ariamh, de bhrí gurbh é amháin a ceadaíodh isteach sa teach le linn dom a bheith ag éirí suas, níorbh eol dom go ceann blianta fada ina dhiaidh sin cé a bhí i bhfeighil na Gaeilge ann. Ba ghnáthach liom an Ghaeilge a léamh i gcónaí ach tá fhios agam go raibh seisean imithe nuair a chuir mé alt isteach ag bréagnú tuairisce, a bhí thar a bheith leataobhach i mo thuairim, i dtaobh an tsaoil in Inis Mór. D'imigh an t-alt ar throigh gan tuairisc agus roinnt éigin blianta ina dhiaidh sin ceapadh mise i mo Eagarthóir Gaeilge ar an bpáipéar.

Mura bhfuil dul amú mór orm, triúr a ghníomhaigh sa bpost idir imeacht Chearbhaill Uí Dhálaigh agus mo theacht féin. Níl aon dul amú orm i dtaobh an laghdú a bhí tagtha ar mhéid an spáis a bhI faoi Ghaeilge le linn an ama chéanna. Bhí sé le cúngú tuilleadh faoi mo réimeas féin is baolach.

Ag an bpointe seo ní raibh aithne curtha agam ar Chearbhaill ach bhí togha na haithne agam ar a dhearthair, Aengus, a bhí ina leabharlannaí i "Scéala Éireann" agus faoina bhfuil seanchas fairsing i measc iriseoirí na linne. Ansin fuaireas cuireadh chun labhairt ag mórchruinniú an Chumainn Gaelach, i gColáiste na Trionóide, an oíche go raibh an Reachtaire ag léamh a pháipéir. Cearbhall Ó Dálaigh a bhí sa gcathaoir.

Rinneamar cuid mhór cainte i ndiaidh an chruinnithe i dtaobh na hiriseoireachta Gaeilge. Tharla go raibh an dearcadh céanna againn ar an ngá a bhí le iriseoireacht bhríomhar, ilghnéitheach a bheith ar súil i nGaeilge, go laethúil dá mb'fhéidir. B'shin a chuir sé roimhe i "Scéala Éireann" nuair a ceapadh ina Eagarthóir Gaeilge é i 1931. Duine ar bith a théann siar ar eagráin tosaidh an nuachtáin feicfidh sé lorg a láimhe sna tuairiscí laethúla ar imeachtaí den uile shórt.

Ní gach Gaeilgeoir a bhí buíoch de. Bhí daoine ann a mheas nár cheart don Ghaeilge drannadh ach amháin le hábhair ón díleann agus nár cheart focal ar bith nach raibh a shean-eire caonach liath air a scaoileadh isteach sa teanga ar chor ar bith.

Mar ba dhual do dhuine a bhí ilteangach le cois a bheith ildánach, níor ghéill Cearbhall Ó Dálaigh do na pisreoga seo. Ba mhór agamsa an uair úd a chomhairle agus a fhocail misnithe. Ní rabhas ach tosaithe ar chéard chleasach agus ba mhinicí i gcomhthionól na Gaeilge san am an cáineadh ná an comhairle.

D'fhág mise freisin Scéala Éireann" ach d'fhan mé leis an gcéard a dfhoghlaim mé ansin agus cé gur ar ócáidí foirmeálta ba mhó a chastaí Cearbhall orm ba í an scríobhneoireacht a tharraingíodh sé anuas i gcónaí. Táim bródúil as an t-aon phictiúir dá bhfuil agam den bheirt againn inéindí, maraon le Mícheál Hartnett agus an tOllamh Eoghan Mac Ciarnáin, nuair a bhronn sé Duais na Fondúireachta Gael-Mheiriceánaigh orm féin agus ar Mhícheál.

Bhí sé casta ar ais ón Eoraip, mar a raibh príomhghradam dlí an Chomhphobail bainte amach aige, agus é ina Uachtarán ar Éirinn. Measaim gur thuig gach mionaicme pobail, lucht léinn, aos ealaíon agus pobal na Gaeilge go raibh Uachtarán againn nach loicfeadh orthu; ar a gcúiseanna agus ar an tír.

Níor loic. Nuair a chonaic sé oifig na hUachtarántachta agus a ionad faoin mBunreacht dá dhíspeagadh, chonaic pobal mór na hÉireann cén miotal a bhí sa bhfear séimh, cúirtéiseach seo. Rinne sé an rud is annamh sa tír seo: sheas sé ar phrionsabal neamhphearsanta, chuir sé tábhacht a oifige roimh an uile ní agus d'éirigh sé as a phost. D'fhág sé breith faoin bpobal agus faoin stair.

San agallamh teilifíse a rinne sé le Prionsias Mac Aonghusa ar *Féach,* tar éis dó éirí as an Uachtarántacht, d'iompair sé é féin leis an ndínit a thug sé ó bhroinn leis agus leis an gcruas intinne a bhain feangadh as na bolamáin béice. Tar éis an chláir ba léir nach raibh fonn air an scéal a phlé tuilleadh ach, ní nach ionadh, bhí an fonn sin go láidir orthu siúd a bhí sa timpeall. Níor cheadaigh sé dó féin ach abairt fhonóideach amháin. Nuair a fiafraíodh de céard a mheas sé ar an gcosaint a bhí déanta ag an Ollamh le Dlí, John M. Kelly, ar iompar an Rialtais ó thaobh an Bhunreachta, dúirt sé, "I think that Kelly's law is definitely an ass".

Tar éis adhlacadh Sheáin Uí Ríordáin a labhair mé go deireannach leis. Chuir sé scata againn faoi gheasa ár n-ómos don Ríordánach a chur ar phár agus a fhoilsiú taobh istigh de bhliain. Ba bheag an cheapadh a bhí againn go mbeadh an dualgas sin le comhlíonadh againn, ina chás féin, chomh luath tar éis an lae sin.

Ní bhíonn aon léamh ar na rudaí sin agus is fearr go mór nach mbeadh. Níl sa leacht áirithe cuimhneacháin seo ach trí choiscéim trócaire na gcarad. D'fhéach sé féin chuige go raibh a ionad sa stair, agus sa seanchas is comhachtaí ná an stair ar intinn an phobail in Éirinn go minic, go raibh sin aimsithe sar ar imigh sé uainn chomh hobann.

AIDAN CARL MATHEWS

TWO SWANS

1. RETURNING TO KILCOOLE

Hubcaps, horsedroppings rubble the sand.
Although I had managed to remember
The fabulous frenzy of alarmed snipe,
Hedges brown as a smoker's fingers,
The railway track was foremost in my mind.

Often in my eagerness, I anklesprained
Among those rails, was always terrified
Of trains running me over, had nightmares
Full of broken skulls, revolving wheels.
I used to go there with my godfather
Who had a blackthorn and noticed everything.

I grew up to his hip, elbow, shoulder:
Then it was time to begin remembering
Important things. The heron we both saw
Through his binoculars when I was twelve
And informed him it was a flamingo;
Or the time we were there around midnight

To hear the ocean perspiring and blacker
Than tar. I suppose I was about fourteen
And needed to be alone, and so we put
Two hundred yards between the two of us.
I think we were closer then than ever before.

2. SAYING GOODBYE

This moment too is ours, is given between us
Brown rain on the window, wind outside:
An asthmatic breathing, drawing breath. I have you
Instants to myself as, even in death,
You conduct the room's silence, compose
A pas-de-deux of light and shadow. Thickly,
The tall, fat candles mope. Through the small hours,
I crouch beside you, and wait to watch
The stomach lift with a taking of breath,
The thin, stitched eyelids stir. But you go out
To a silence that I cannot overhear,
A rumour of hearsay. I have left
Only — *More light!* — the moisture of phrases.

Later, hours before the light, I hear
The plain chant of the blackbird,
Urbi et orbe! The morning prays in Greek,
Its sunlight heals the window-pane, picks out,
Illumines on a writing desk beside me
A traveller's copy of St. John's gospel,
A penguin edition of Plato's *Phaedo*,
And a folio of poems that I gave you
En route to China. From that Middle Kingdom,
You wrote to tell me of a blue pagoda. Now,
What can I give you but, in grief and longing,
Silence of words at the storm-centre,
A wildflower pressed in the book of your leaving?

And light blazes, is out of control! I touch,
Homing on the distance of your dying,
Pianist's fingers on a hand-carved Christ,
Until I come of age. You who taught me
The gaiety of reverence, teach me now
The inheritance of my loss, inhabit
My heart intensely. Cearbhall, your face
Fades to a watermark on all my papers,
And a paperweight. I would labour to prise
A may-day from this moment, strive
To give it flesh by turning it to stone.
And still I borrow from you, knowing well
You have given me, again, this moment too.

EIBHLÍN NÍ BHRIAIN

FEAR AR ROTHAR

Impire ar uaisleacht, Guaire ar oineach. Is mó a airimid uainn anois é ná riamh. Ní léir dúinn an uaisleacht i saol na hÉireann ó cailleadh Cearbhall Ó Dálaigh. An chéad uair a labhair sé leis an bpobal mar Uachtarán mhol sé an rothar i saol na hÉireann. I gCaisleán Bhaile Átha Cliath a bhí sé ag caint tar éis dó dualgaisí na hUachtaránachta a ghlacadh air féin. An uair dheireannach beagnach ar labhair sé liom bhí sé ag moladh an rothar i saol na Síne. Bhí sé de phribhiléid agam agallamh a dhéanamh leis an Dálach tar éis dó filleadh ón tSín. B'fhéidir go raibh sé ró-shoineanta, ach ní bhfuair sé locht ar bith ar thír nach raibh cárr ná teilifís ag éinne inti ach teach agus obair ag chuille dhuine agus rothar ag a bhformhór mór.

Na pástí beaga sa scoil Ghaeltachta i mBéal Feirste, bhí a pheictiúir crochta ar an mballa acu, é ag marcaíocht ar mhuin rothair. Ní raibh fhios acu riamh roimhe sin, adeir siad liom, go raibh daoine móra mar Uachtaráin ar an saol a raibh Gaeilge acu.

Siombail chuí ab ea an rothar sin; níl meas anois ar fhear an rothair; ní tugtar meas a thuilleadh ach d'fhear an Mhercedes mhóir.

An saibhir agus an daibhir b'ionann iad i láthair an Uachtaráin. An té a thuig a chéard — Mícheál Mac Liammóir, Siobhán Nic Cionnaith — b'iad seo na daoine a thuil gean an Uachtaráin. An fear Gaeltachta — Donnchadh Shéamuis Ó Drisceoil ag fáiltiú roimh Uachtarán na hÉireann ar an gcé in Oileán Chléire, an tUachtarán ag breith barróige air, an bheirt fhear ag iomaíocht ar feadh an lae agus na filí iomadúla de chlainn Dálaigh faoi chaibidil acu — is do Dhonncadh Shéamuis na Gaeltachta a thug an tUachtarán Ó Dálaigh urraim. Ach duine ar bith a thug grá don nGaeilge agus a rinne a chuid féin di — na páistí sa scoil i mBéal Feirste a fuair cuireadh ar leith chuig Áras an Uachtaráin, an saighdiúirín singil a bhí ina ábhar ginearála dar leis an Uachtarán nuair a bhronn sé fáinne air ina bhaile dhúchais, Brí Cualann — b'iad seo an mhuintir thar éinne eile ar dhromchla an domhain a chuir áthas ar a chroí.

Mórtas cine a bhí orm agus mé ag breathnú ar an Uachtarán Ó Dálaigh agus a bhean agus iad ar chuairt Stáit chun na Fraince. Agus níor ghá dhuit bheith ró-eolach le nod a bhaint as turas "príobháideach" na beirte nuair a bhí deireadh leis an gcuairt Stáit: go háiteacha a bhain le Jeanne d'Arc, an Marechale Saxe agus Máire Stíobhart.

Ní fiú bheith ag trácht a thuilleadh ar na daoine a threascair an tUachtarán. Thug an pobal a mbreith orthu sin lá an toghcháin. Truaillíodh muid go léir an uair sin, ach déantar dearmad anois ar an ísealaicme úd. Bíodh cuimhne againn feasta ar an sárfhear a bhí i gceannas orainn ar feadh ré narbh fhada, ach ré a thál torad céadtach. Mar a dúirt Eoghan Ó Néill de chuid Chomhdháil Náisiúnta na Gaeilge: dá mbeadh uait fear a chruthú d'Uachtaránacht na hÉireann, sé Cearbhall Ó Dálaigh a chruthófá.

An uair dheireannach a chonacas é, b'ar shochraid Mhichíl Mhic Liammóir é. Bhí an Dálach ag labhairt cois uaighe a charad faoi scáth Bhinn Éadair agus d'fhéadfá Diarmaid agus Gráinne agus Aonghus an Ghrá a shamhladh á chaoineadh. Bhí siad sin agus Fionn agus seacht gcatha na Féinne ag géarchaoineadh sa Snaidhm Diardaoin Manndála, lá sneachta agus gála, agus Cearbhall Ó Dálaigh á chur faoin bhfód. Bhí bá an phobail Fhódhlaigh lena bhaintreach, Máirín. Bhí Éire uile ina baintreach an lá sin.

CATHAL BUÍ MAC GIOLLA GUNNA

AN BONNÁN BUÍ

THOMAS KINSELLA

THE YELLOW BITTERN

A bhonnáin bhuí, is é mo chrá do luí
is do chnámha críon tar éis a gcreim,
is chan díobháil bídh ach easpa dí
d'fhág tú 'do luí ar chúl do chinn;
is measa liom féin ná scrios na Traí
thú bheith sínte ar leacaibh lom,
is nach ndearna tú díth ná dolaidh is tír
is nárbh fhearr leat fíon ná uisce poill.

Is a bhonnáin álainn, mo mhíle crá
do chúl ar lár amuigh insa tslí,
is gur moch gach lá a chluininn do ghráig
ar an láib agus tú ag ól na dí;
is é an ní adeir cách le do dheartháir Cathal
go bhfaighidh mé bás mar súd, más fíor;
ní hamhlaidh atá — súd an préachan breá
chuaigh a dh'éag ar ball, gan aon bhraon dí.

A bhonnáin óig, is é mo mhíle brón
thú bheith romham i measc na dtom,
is na lucha móra ag triall chun do thórraimh
ag déanamh spóirt is pléisiúir ann;
dá gcuirfeá scéala is am fá mo dhéinse
go raibh tú i ngéibheann nó i mbróid fá dheoch,
do bhrisfinn béim ar an loch sin Vesey
a fhliuchfadh do bhéal is do chorp isteach.

Ní hé bhur n-éanlaith atá mise ag éagnach,
an lon, an smaolach, ná an chorr ghlas —
ach mo bhonnán buí a bhí lán den chroí,
is gur cosúil liom féin é ina ghné is a dhath;
bhíodh sé choíche ag síoról na dí,
agus deir na daoine go mbím mar sin seal,
is níl deor dá bhfaighead nach ligfead síos
ar eagla go bhfaighinnse bás den tart.

Dúirt mo stór liom ligean den ól
nó nach mbeinnse beo ach seal beag gearr,
ach dúirt mé léi go dtug sí bréag
is gurbh fhaide mo shaolsa an deoch úd a fháil;
nach bhfaca sibh éan an phíobáin réidh
a chuaigh a dh'éag den tart ar ball? —
a chomharsain chléibh, fliuchaidh bhur mbéal,
óir chan fhaigheann sibh braon i ndiaidh bhur mbáis.

Bittern, I'm sorry to see you stretched
with your bones decayed and eaten away.
Not want of food but need of a drink
has brought you so to lie face up.
I feel it worse than the ruin of Troy
to see you stretched on the naked stones,
who caused no hurt nor harm in the world,
as happy with boghole water as wine.

It hurts, fair bittern, a thousandfold
— your fallen head on the open road,
whose honk I heard in the early mornings
out on the mud as you took your drink.
Everyone tells your brother Cathal
that's certainly how I'm going to die.
Not so. Behold this handsome bird
lately dead for want of a drop.

Sorrow, young bittern, a thousandfold
to see you before me among the clumps,
and the big rats travelling toward your wake,
taking part in the fun and games.
If only you'd sent me word in time
that you were in trouble and needed a drink
I'd have dealt a blow at Vesey's lake
would have wetted your mouth and your innards too.

Your other birds I don't lament,
blackbird, thrush, or the grey crane,
but my yellow bittern full of heart
so like myself in face and hue.
He was for ever taking a drink
and they say I'm the same from time to time
— but I'll leave undrunk no drop I find
for fear I'd catch my death of thirst.

My darling said give up the drink
or I've only a little while to live
but I told her that she told a lie,
the selfsame drink prolongs my life.
Have ye not seen this smooth-necked bird
that died of thirst a while ago?
Wet your lips, my neighbours dear.
There won't be a drop when you're dead and gone.

ISAAC COHEN

COMMUNITY SPIRIT

Cearbhall Ó Dálaigh will be remembered as a brilliant Irish scholar, jurist and humanitarian, who brought honour and distinction to the Irish nation. He possessed the ability to inspire the hearts of all Irish men and women, who gladly responded to his sincere and humble approach, and were prepared to grasp his warm hand of brotherly respect and friendship. He represented the best of modern and historic Gaelic culture, and was the product of the finest achievements of European civilisation.

The Jewish community in Ireland shared to the full the widespread love of this prince of humanity, and they were grieved at the loss of a great man whom they were proud to regard as a personal friend.

During the period of my Chief Rabbinate in Ireland, I had many occasions to come into contact with Mr. Ó Dálaigh and to observe his brilliant achievements, at first during his Presidency of the Irish Supreme Court, and later as President of the Republic of Ireland. Many members of the Jewish community remembered him with affection from his student days and his successful career at the Irish Bar. In whatever part of Ireland he found himself, whether in the busy academic or industrial life of Dublin, or the peaceful vistas of Co. Kerry, or the rugged mountainous Gaeltacht, Cearbhall Ó Dálaigh was the happy local boy who had made good and who deserved to be respected.

As a young man, Cearbhall Ó Dálaigh came into contact with a number of Jewish families who lived at the time on and around the Dublin South Circular Road. He was greatly impressed by the traditional character-traits of the Jewish community: their family life, their industriousness, their devotion to religious observance, and their love of learning. He admired the diligence of his fellow Jewish students at the Christian Brothers' School where he was a pupil, and he became acquainted with some of their customs. He used to relate with pride how he would gladly visit a Jewish home on a Saturday morning in order to help the religiously observant family overcome some of their Sabbath restrictions, such as the Biblical prohibition of making fire on the Sabbath day, by himself adjusting the light and heating for the Jewish family, since he, as a non-Jew, was not placed under any such restraints.

In later years he followed with deepest sympathy the tragedy of Jewish persecution in Nazi Europe, and he rejoiced with the Jewish people when they strenuously built for themselves a free home-land in the land of Israel. As an outstanding European jurisprudentialist, he eagerly accepted the invitation of the Hebrew University in Jerusalem to deliver a highly acclaimed course of lectures in its Law Faculty. It was most appropriate that after his death the Jewish community in Dublin endowed a splendid lecture-hall in his memory in the Law Faculty of that same University. President Ó Dálaigh had himself been most deeply impressed by the breathtaking view from the University terrace across to the Dead Sea and the biblical mountains of Moab looming in the background.

As President of Ireland, Cearbhall Ó Dálaigh was conscious not only of his constitutional responsibilities, which he honoured with meticulous care, but also of his opportunity of uniting all sections of the nation with a common bond of mutual respect and understanding. He was ready to serve his people in any possible manner, and when he made the call to "community spirit" the theme of his leadership of the nation he took up the task in hand with unselfish dedication. Just as throughout his tenure of office as President of the Supreme Court he played a decisive part in upholding the rights of the individual citizen in a number of significant judgments, so as President he devoted his energies to engaging in the widely diversified cultural interests of the Irish people. His personality as President could be compared with the choice of David by the prophet Samuel: "The Lord hath sought Him a man after His own heart; and the Lord hath appointed him a Prince over His people".

An example of his courtesy and humility presented itself particularly on an occasion when he invited my wife and myself to tea at Arus an Uachtaráin. He was fully aware that, according to Jewish religious practice, it would not be fitting to offer an observant Jew items of food prohibited by dietary law. When we arrived, I was most pleasantly surprised to find that, out of consideration for the religious scruples of his guests, he had personally obtained each item of food on the table from the duly authorised purveyors of Kosher food, whose shops he had visited that day in the old Jewish neighbourhood he knew so well around the South Circular Road. The warm, attentive hospitality of himself and his charming wife, Máirín, was beautifully reminiscent of the Biblical injunction to "love thy neighbour as thy self".

As a jurist of international repute, Cearbhall Ó Dálaigh was not content with his vast knowledge of the Irish, English and Roman legal systems. His search for knowledge drove him to study the organisation of other legal systems, embracing at the same time the philosophical, social and religious backgrounds of each one. he made himself fully conversant with the different systems of European law, both ancient and contemporary. He often spoke with extensive knowledge of the impressive system of Brehon law in early Irish history.

Likewise, in the course of his studies in Comparative Law, he gained a considerable insight into the principles of Jewish law as developed in the juristic writings of the Talmud. He realised that, apart from early Biblical law, Jewish Rabbinic law in the Third Century (the period of Roman Law's notable development) had already achieved an elaborate legal system, one which continued uninterruptedly until the present day. It was therefore with obvious pleasure and knowledge that, as Chief Justice of Ireland, Judge Ó Dálaigh presided at a public lecture, under the auspices of the Chief Rabbinate of Ireland, on "Leading Concepts of Jewish Law", given by Rabbi K. Kahana, the professor of Talmud at the London Jews' College. In his opening address, Mr. Ó Dálaigh demonstrated a remarkable grasp of those concepts, and described their importance in the understanding of Comparative Law.

His visit to China inspired him to engage in a study of Chinese thought and culture. Always the enthusiastic student, he was exhilarated by his new experience. When I heard him open the magnificent exhibition of Oriental Art and Manuscripts at the Chester Beatty library, I could not help being inspired by his natural exuberance and his admiration of the beauty of ancient Chinese civilisation. His address on China and the Orient was no exceptional performance on his part. He was always happy to expound on any subject with an eager and almost childlike enthusiasm which captured all his delighted listeners.

The concern of President Ó Dálaigh to embrace with respect every section of Irish public life was superbly expressed by his personal attendance at the Special Divine Service for the Inauguration of the President held by the Jewish community in the Adelaide Road Synagogue, Dublin, in addition to the national Service held in the Cathedral on the same day. According to Jewish practice, he was received by the elders of the community, and the Congregation pronounced the traditional benediction to the Almighty on the occasion of greeting a King, a scholar and a man of righteousness. The benediction proclaimed: "Blessed be He who hath bestowed of His own glory upon His human creations". In greeting the new President, I quoted the noble words of John Milton: "Behold this God-fearing man, 'erect with native honour clad'". In my homily, I described the seven qualifications enumerated by the Jewish philosopher Maimonides as the prerequisites of any judge according to Jewish law: wisdom, humility, the fear of God, hatred of gain, love of truth, amiability, and a reputation above reproach. President Ó Dálaigh, I said, was a worthy example of one who possessed all these qualities.

I concluded my Address on this historic occasion by bestowing on the President the traditional priestly blessing, "The Lord bless thee and keep thee. . .", which I delivered in its original biblical form in the Hebrew language, followed by its translation into Irish. In all the three hundred year history of the presence of Jews in Ireland, this was the first time that the Irish blessing had ever been pronounced from the pulpit in a Jewish Synagogue.

His sad and untimely death was a grievous loss to Ireland and to all those whom he loved. He was a light to the nations, and his death leaves a void that cannot easily be filled; but his soul will now for ever rest in peace.

JOHN MONTAGUE

A RESIGNED PRESIDENT

Cearbhall Ó Dálaigh's smile reinstated words like goodness, gentleness, generosity, words that had lost their meaning, crudely devalued. And I think such qualities attract hatred from the unbelieving, the cynical.

On a summer evening, beyond Sneem,
we discuss your resignation,
the memoir you hoped to write. Again
I observe your gentleness,
that absence of meanness, or of malice
which left you helpless

Before the silent bite of the terrier
with his small teeth,
the arid legality of the Law Professor,
putting you in your place,
who held our highest, where honour shines,
a credit to our race.

We joke lightly about your bardic name,
a disgrace to the Ó Dálaighs,
you laughed, *not even a poor poet,*
and I felt the shame
of your being slighted by a Maenad
citing Dante's Celestine.

Holy Thursday. As in the old dispensation
we saw the floodgates open,
that same valley cowled in mourning
as your resigned body
was laid down, the spirit leaping towards
the light you believed in.

All night blue flames flickered in
the de Vere stained glass
above the high altar, the oak coffin
and in the chill morning
hosts assemble across Ireland to attend him,
like a murdered king.

With Chopin's funeral march resounding in
the hushed streets of Sneem
that watchful ring of snowy mountains
a solemn salute of guns
as a still young nation comes to attention
to honour him.

But military pomp and precision dwindle
in the wind's fierce requiem.
As Hillery speaks, the fury of the rain
hardens to hail:
our land's grief is manifest; they offended us,
offending him.

Cearbhall, *duine uasal,* open minded Christian,
generous, unjudging spirit,
your merry smile made all the clichés true:
blossom of the sweet branch,
delightful, for a summer while, to have broken
bread with you

who spoke over Ó Riordáin, who spoke over Seán
in St. Gobnait's of Ballyvourney,
and now you have joined that ghostly procession
always moving on
from our still unresolved republic of pain,
restating the problem.

BRENDAN SMITH

THE GREAT TENT HAS COLLAPSED

Cearbhall Ó Dálaigh joined the Council of the Dublin Theatre Festival early in the 1960s and was immediately elected a Vice-Chairman of that body. At the time, he was Chief Justice and had already become known as a patron of the arts. When he was appointed to the European Court, he kept in touch with all the progress and all the problems of the Dublin Theatre Festival.

On returning to the country to become President of Ireland, he had to resign the Vice-Chairmanship of the Festival Council, but there was no doubt of his abiding interest in the Festival events. He set an example to the whole community by attending not alone every production on the main programme but also many items of the fringe programme each year during his Presidency. The overseas press made general comment on the fact that they had never seen a Head of State anywhere show such a deep personal interest in the theatre. Moreover, he felt so strongly about the Festival that he helped in its continuation in ways that will never be revealed. His charm of manner, his understanding of the artists' problems, and his readiness to help them, revealed his innate sensitivity.

One could make the mistake occasionally of assuming that this sensitivity and gentleness added up to a form of weakness. Those who made this error quickly found that behind such gentleness lay a rock of carefully wrought wisdom. He could not and would not be rushed to a decision or opinion that was unjust to any other person. Within my experience, I have only known him to be provoked to anger on one occasion — and I was the culprit! In my blinkered enthusiasm, I had expressed an opinion that did not take into consideration his own view or that of a concerned third party. When I hastened to apologise, he was quick to respond with typical good humour. I think that this particular exchange did much to cement what proved to be an enduring friendship.

Theatre in any and every form he attended with delight and concentrated involvement: tragedy, comedy, farce, grand operas, musicals, ballet, mime. Not content with theatre-going, I remember his secretary 'phoning from the Aras one day during a Festival: could I verify that one of the famous Irish circuses was performing just outside Dublin? I confirmed this, and was asked to have two ringside seats reserved for him that evening. I will never forget the excitement with which the Fossett family reacted to this news. Neither will I forget President Ó Dálaigh's delighted participation during the performance. At the interval, he expressed a desire to meet all the performers, both human and animal, after the show. Many tears of joy were shed that night under the Big Top and, later, in the caravan home of the Fossett family when the President joined them for tea and fruitcake. Mr. Fossett's sole regret was that President Ó Dálaigh had insisted on paying for his seats!

I remember an amusing incident in which Cearbhall Ó Dálaigh was involved during the Theatre Festival. He was attending a play at the Eblana Theatre on the same night as Michael Scott, the internationally known and honoured architect, whose many projects include the design of Busarus, the Central Bus Station in the basement of which the Eblana is situated. After the performance, President Ó Dálaigh walked up towards the main entrance with Michael Scott and myself. At the main portico, he pointed to a polished stone insertion in the red brick-work, and said quite innocently, "That's very attractive, Michael; but what exactly is it for?' The architect's face creased into a smile.

"Well, Mr. President, when this portico was nearing completion, I remembered that this type of brick can be sensitive to pressurised heat, even to body heat. I knew well that buildings like Busarus seem to attract characters who love to pass the time by lounging against attractive brick-work, chatting away the hours and possibly regaling visitors with stories of old Dublin. Some of these characters leave a permanent impression on the bricks. I thought that by inserting a recessed, reasonably ornate, polished lean-to, it would protect at least this corner of the building".

I never saw Cearbhall Ó Dálaigh laugh more heartily as he tried it for size.

A final Festival story. On a later occasion, after a first night performance, I found that the President had diverted his car to the Festival Club at the Tailors' Hall, a restored guild-hall in the Liberties. All the rooms were fully occupied by playwrights, actors, actresses, designers, directors, theatre-goers, and journalists. One room alone had no bar-service. This was the "talking-shop" where tea, coffee, and other non-alcoholic refreshments were available. There I found the President, the inevitable cup of tea in his hand, in his element: chatting with artistes and technicians from every theatrical venue in Dublin. To my dismay, I also saw two well-known political journalists approaching him. At that time, the President had exercised a constitutional prerogative which had aroused public interest and controversy; and I feared that the journalists would try to take advantage of his presence by questioning him. In spite of appeals from myself and others not to do so, I was reminded that the President had himself been a professional journalist in his younger days. And, in the event, a very lucid exposition of the President's constitutional position was provided by the President himself.

In all matters on which he had to give judgment or opinion, Cearbhall Ó Dálaigh always reseached the subject thoroughly beforehand. For that reason, authors, actors, actresses, and directors welcomed the after-show chat with him. He had, too, a gift for making criticism sound like a compliment. I recall his visit to the world-premiere of Stewart Parker's play, *Spokesong,* at the Dublin Theatre Festival in 1975. The play concerns the whole story of the bicycle, in a Belfast context. The President spoke with Stewart at the interval and, even though the play had barely reached its half-way point, Cearbhall was not only in love with the script but with the playing and with the subject itself, an enthusiasm he obviously shared with the playwright. Stewart, who was meeting the President for the first time, was astounded at his knowledge of the beginnings of the bicycle and of the personal history of John Boyd Dunlop, the Belfast man who invented the pneumatic tyre.

A master of many languages, Cearbhall Ó Dálaigh never shirked undertaking a new tongue, particularly if international courtesy called for it. I remember him rising to address a Theatre Festival gathering which included visitors from many lands, and greeting them in Gaelic, English, French, Italian, German, Danish, Icelandic, and a North African dialect.

My memory flows over with stories about this quite remarkable man. As long as the powers of memory stay with me, I will always remember him as a person of profound judgment and intellect, rich in humour, compassion, and integrity.

PAUL DURCAN

LAMENT FOR CEARBHALL Ó DÁLAIGH

Into a simple grave six feet deep,
Next grave to a Kerry sheep farmer,
Your plain oak coffin was laid
In a hail of hail:
The gods in the Macgillycuddy's Reeks
(Snow on their summits)
Were in a white, dancing rage
Together with the two don-
Keys who would not budge
From the graveyard,
And the poets and the painters,
The actors and the actresses,
The etchers and the sculptors,
The child-singers — those multiplying few
Who, despite the ever darkening night
Believe with their hearts' might
As did you
In a spoken music of the utter earth:

You who, for a brief hour,
Were Chieftain of a Rising People;
Who brought back into Tara's Halls
The blind poets and the blinder harpists;
Who, the brief hour barely ended,
Were insulted massively,
Betrayed most viciously
By a monstrous bourgeoisie;
And, worse by far,
By *la trahaison des clercs*;
Where were those talented men
In the government of the talents
When the jackbooted
Bourgeois crackled the whip?
The talented men kept their silence,
Their souls committed to finance;
Now hear their mouth-traps snap shut:
"No comment, no comment, no comment, no comment".

Ah, Cearbhall, but in your death
You led them all a merry dance:
Hauling them all out of their soft Dublin haunts,
Out of their Slickness and Glickness,
Out of their Snugvilles and Smugtowns,
You had them travel all the long,
Long way down to Sneem:
Sneem of the Beautiful Knot.
By God and by Dana,
Cearbhall, forgive me
But it was a joy to watch them
With their wind-flayed faces
Getting all knotted-up
In the knot of your funeral;
Wind, rain, hail, and sleet,
Were on your side
And spears of sunlight
Who, like yourself, have never lied.
Blue Lightning
And Thunder written on the mountaintops
And Disgrace on the traitors' faces.

In all our memories, Cearbhall,
You will remain as fresh
As the green rock jutting up
In mid-stream
Where fresh and salt waters meet
Under the Bridge at Sneem.

How the respectability squirmed
In the church when beside your coffin
The Ó Riada choir sang pagan laments
For their dead Chieftain.
"O he is my hero, my brave loved one".
Papal Nuncio, Bishops,
Passed wind in their misericords,
Their stony faces expressionless.

A Gaelic Chinaman whose birthplace
At 85 Main Street, Bray,
Is now a Chinese Restaurant
("The Jasmine", owned by Chi Leung Nam):
O tan-man smiling on the mountain,
You are gone from us now, O Yellow Sun.
Small laughing man,
Cearbhall of the merry eyes,
A Gaelic Charlie Chaplin who became
Chief Justice and President,
Hear our mute confessions now:
We were afraid of the man that licks
Life with such relish;
We were not up to your tricks,
Did not deserve you, Cearbhall
Of the City-Centre and the Mountain-Pool:
Príomh Breitheamh, tUachtarán: Slán.

SIOBHÁN MCKENNA

NÍ CRÍOCH ACH ATH-FHÁS: NOT THE FINISH BUT REBIRTH

As I look out my window, I see a wet cold windy day. On just such a day, Cearbhall Ó Dálaigh, former President of Ireland, was buried in a remote corner of County Kerry. "Happy the corpse the rain falls on". That day, the little village of Sneem was thronged with people from all walks of life. Hailstones as well as tears stung the mourners' faces. The local people stood grave and silent outside their church to leave room for the strangers from Dublin and other foreign parts. We had lost a marvellous man.

Inside, the church was freezing. I found myself sitting beside Frank Aiken, an old friend of Cearbhall, who greeted me in Irish and then took off his overcoat to share it with me. The Cúil Aodha choir had arrived from County Cork to sing Seán O'Riada's Mass in Irish. Cearbhall would have been pleased. The all-male voices, a mixture of young and old, sang out the verses of an old anonymous prayer:

Ag Críost an síol	With Christ the seed
Ag Críost an Fóghmhar	With Christ the harvest
I n-iothlainn Dé	In God's granary
Go dtugtar sinn.	May we be brought.
Ag Críost an mhuir	With Christ the sea
Ag Críost an t-iasc	With Christ the fish
I líontaibh Dé	In God's nets
Go gcastar sinn.	May we meet.
Ó fhás go h-aois	From growth to age
Is ó aois go bás	And from age to death
Do dhá láimh a Chríost	Thy two hands, O Christ,
Anall tharainn.	Be about us.

Ó bhás go críoch	From death to the finish
Ní críoch ach ath-fhás	Not the finish but re-birth
I bParrthas na ngrást	In the Paradise of grace
Go rabhmid.	May we be.

When Mass had ended, Máirín, Cearbhall's wife, bowed her head in appreciation to the choir before she turned to leave. It was a kind, thoughtful gesture on her day of mourning. It was the sort of gesture which brought to mind the great kindness of her husband. Kindness sprang from Cearbhall like water from a well.

As we filed out of the church at Sneem, I remembered a very different kind of day in another small town in Ireland — Coillte Magh in County Mayo. It was a joyous occasion. The sun shone. The streets were decorated with gay bunting and the red carpet was down to greet the President. We were celebrating the poet Raftery's birthday. I had been invited down to read some of his poems, so I was going over them when Cearbhall arrived. I knew his arrival would not be a noisy one. Still, I was surprised when someone knocked on my door to say that the President was downstairs and could I join the other guests.

The parlour on the ground floor was crowded but as all eyes were turned in one direction I knew that the gentleman with his head stuck out the window surrounded by dozens of excited children could be none other than Cearbhall. One little girl in particular seemed determined to gain the President's ear. Cearbhall withdrew into the room and made straight for the Canon who was elderly, and, judging from the way he cupped his hand around his ear, appeared a little hard of hearing. Presently the Canon nodded his head up and down. Then there was another whisper from the President, another nod from the Canon, yet another whisper, then a final nod. Cearbhall returned to the window and leaned out to the little girl. There were cheers from the children when they learned that the President had persuaded the Canon to give them three days holiday from school. Later the President gave a scholarly and meticulously researched talk on Raftery.

Cearbhall always created a quiet kind of excitement when he was President. People always seemed so pleased with him and happy. As he left Coillte Magh that evening the whole town appeared to be outside the hotel to wave him good-bye.

In Sneem, as the hearse went up the hill to the Main Street, old countrymen stood bare-headed in the rain. The women's lips moved in prayer. Outside the town, a long narrow country lane, clearly not designed for state funerals, led to the grave-yard. Ambassadors, poets, politicians, writers, teachers, theatre people, farmers, fishermen, shopkeepers, journalists, children tramped through the mud. Crowds standing on the hillsides, unable to hear the oration by President Hillery because of the wind and rain, began to talk among themselves. The local schoolmaster told me how he had 'phoned Cearbhall to say how honoured the school would be if he could spare the time to visit. The teacher was a Latin enthusiast and mentioned how disappointing it was to find such a lack of interest in the subject today. No sooner said than done. I gathered that Cearbhall arrived to give a lesson in Latin, and succeeded in drumming up considerable enthusiasm in the pupils. This story particularly intrigued me: Cearbhall the continuous scholar, the continuous student, the continuous teacher.

Cearbhall was deeply involved with people and most accessible. He was very much at home with us actors as we were with him. He was a genuine and frequent theatre-goer and liked to discuss the play with us afterwards. I remember, during his European appointment, I was playing Juno at the Mermaid Theatre in London. My friend Sean Kenny had directed me in the part in Toronto previously and was to have directed the London production. Sean died tragically on the very morning rehearsals were due to begin, and the producer, Sir Bernard Miles, insisted that I take over the direction as well as playing the part of Juno. It was a nerve-wracking experience. Cearbhall read about the production on his way back to Dublin for a visit, and broke his journey in London. It was Sunday. He arrived with his arms full of roses he had bought at a street corner. Afterwards, his enthusiasm for the production (we had Sean's set) and his warm words of praise for the performances did much to console us for our loss of Sean. He was very considerate.

When Cearbhall resigned from the Presidency and went to live in Kerry, I feared the theatre would lose him, but he was to remain a faithful playgoer to the end. The last time we met was when I was playing Sarah Bernhardt in *Memoir* at the Olympia theatre in Dublin. He travelled up from Kerry that day, returning the same night. My last communication with him was when I received flowers and a message from him for the opening night of the same play in London. He was in hospital. Little did I think that the next exchange of flowers would be for his grave.

Ar dheis Dé a anam dílis.

CEARBHALL Ó DÁLAIGH

Born February 12th, 1911.

Educated at Bray National School; Scoil na Leanbh, Ring, Co. Waterford; Synge Street C.B.S., Dublin.

B.A. in Celtic Studies from U.C.D., 1931.

Founded An Cumann Gaelach in U.C.D.
Auditor of the Literary and Historical Society, U.C.D., 1930.

Irish Editor, *The Irish Press*, 1931-1940.

Called to the Irish Bar, 1934.

Married Máirín Nic Dhiarmada in 1934.

Attorney General, 1946-1948, 1951-53.

Judge of the Supreme Court, 1953-1961.

Chief Justice, 1961-1973.

Judge of the Court of Justice of the European Communities, 1973-74.

President of Ireland, 1974-1976.

Died March 21st 1978.

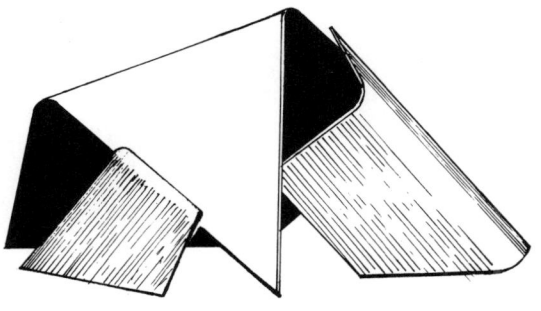

THE MEMORIAL

The Trustees of the Cearbhall Ó Dálaigh Memorial Fund invited a number of distinguished people from the artistic world to form an Artistic Advisory Committee to select an Irish artist of achievement to create a commemorative work sited in Sneem, County Kerry, where Cearbhall Ó Dálaigh and his wife decided to live in retirement.

Vivienne Roche was the chosen artist, and she has created an abstract sculpture in steel, 7′ 3″ high, to be set in the Square at Sneem, of which she writes,

> The initial shell-like image led me to think in terms of working with the sea, specifically with wave-action . . . becoming intensely interested in the infolded interior created by the thrusting plane of the wave . . . gradually the forms emerged . . . reminiscent of mountains and megalithic structures.
>
> I felt that colour should be a major element . . . I decided to paint the interior planes definite colours devised from the colours of the surrounding hills . . . these give the interior a solid, earth-bound mysterious quality, while the exterior is lightened by warm white which also enhances the clean lines and tensile strength of the steel . . . the piece derives much of its interest from the interplay of light and shadow on and through it.

The Memorial was unveiled by Patrick Hillery, President of Ireland, on Sunday 5 June 1983.